To Sandra,

a very speci...

...nd is appreciated by many ......, you
...tinule to bless people with your
...dication in helping others. May your
...e continule to grow, and God bless it
...d guide your future.

From our Family
George Rome Eckerana

MW00625983

BEYOND COMA

PATRICIA ECHEVARRIA

VANTAGE PRESS
New York

Copyright © 1998 by Patricia Echevarria

Published by Vantage Press, Inc.
516 West 34th Street, New York, New York 10001

Manufactured in the United States of America
ISBN: 0-533-12457-3

Library of Congress Catalog Card No.: 97-90683

0 9 8 7 6 5 4 3 2 1

To Israel, my only son, who robbed death for another chance at life; my husband, who believed in God and loved his family; my daughter Michelle, who continues to shine like a princess in a fairytale book; to my Christian friend, Carol, for her loyalty and courage, to my family; and to the testimony of the Lord and His great love.

Is anything too hard for the Lord? At the time appointed "I will return unto thee," according to the time of life.—Genesis 18:14

Contents

Preface

Poems by Those Who Believe in Life

In August, 1992, my son Israel was ejected out of a pickup truck, placed on life-support in a vegetative state, and spent three months in a coma. These poems were written by his family or those close to his family before and after his recovery began and continues.

Offspring of the past, pregnant with the future, the present moment, nevertheless, always exists in eternity, always in eternity as the point of intersection between time and the timelessness of faith, and therefore, as the moment of freedom from past and future.

Thou who art over us,
Thou who art one of us,
Thou who art
Also within us,
May all see Thee—in me also
May I prepare the way for Thee,
May I thank Thee for all that shall fall to my lot,
May I also not forget the needs of others,
Keep me in Thy Love.
As Thou wouldest that all should be kept in mine,
May everything in this my being be directed to Thy
    glory,
And may I never despair.
For I am under Thy hand,
And in Thee is all power and goodness.

Give me a pure heart—that I may see Thee,
A humble heart that I may hear Thee,
A heart of love that I may serve Thee,
A heart of faith that I may abide in Thee,

The "unheard of to be in the hands God,"
Once again a reminder that this is all that remains for
You to live for and once more the feeling of
Disappointment which shows how slow you are to
    learn.

—Dag Hammarskjöld

1

Angels and Dreams

It was cold outside as we rushed to the hospital, and being apprehensive about childbirth, I leaned heavily on George's arm for emotional support, more than for balancing the weight I was carrying. I comforted myself and assumed it was due to being only twenty years old and having my first child. The snow was deep and the sky was gray, and November was not the season in cold Minnesota for feeling secure, for storms had plagued us for weeks.

As we entered the hospital, I knew something was different in my body and this would be the day I would have my first child. I was hoping the doctor would keep his promise and give me assistance for pain as I was not educated in the Lamaze method for birth preparation. After eight hours of unbearable panic and pain, I felt guilty I had grabbed the nurse and my husband both, tearing at their clothes and his hair. We delivered a seven pound boy, and my firstborn son was named Israel. As George watched the baby's head coming through the birth canal, he was relieved, and smiled.

I had spent the last months of my pregnancy seeking a name for him. I had had no ultrasound, but I somehow knew it would be a boy. As I had become enlightened by God a year earlier, somehow my life had changed dramatically in my discernment and realities of the love of God in my life. I felt spiritually sensitive and was pressed to search the Scriptures for a name so I could commit my child to God.

A month before the delivery, I had a dream, and the Scriptures came to me, in Genesis 32, verses 24 to 28 speaking to me of Jacob wrestling with the angel:

As Jacob was left alone, there wrestled with him a man, until the breaking of day. And the man said: Let me go! and Jacob said I will not let you go except you bless me! And the man, (angelic) asked Jacob his name, and asked what Jacob wanted from him. Jacob answered: I will not let you go until you bless me! And the angel said: Your name shall no longer be Jacob, but Israel for you have prevailed with God and man and you will be blessed. The angel maimed the right hip before Jacob let him go and throughout the land Israel now limped as a sign to the people of Israel.

In the late afternoon, I had two more hours to finish the day, as my mind focused on a late client, sitting in front of me with colors and textures of window coverings to select for her new home. I was anxious to finish and process the order for the evening. It had been a long day and closing time was at 8:00 P.M., an hour away. As I offered my best opinion on the information I was given and the sales that were available, my mind drifted back to an hour earlier. "I love you, Mom!" I thought about my son as he dropped by the store before he went to the beach with friends, and remembered the kiss he gave me on the cheek, and his playful personality and sensitive nature. It warmed me and made my spirit proud that I was his mom, and contemplated eighteen years of raising him.

The phone rang over and over again, and I skillfully answered both phones, putting one of them on hold. I ended both conversations with a stressful thought, and scrambled to close the daily sales.

The phone rang again and my husband informed me we were being contacted by the Ventura County Hospital and that I should call the number they gave him, as there was an emergency concerning Israel. I panicked and returned the call. They urged me to come immediately to the emergency room where Israel was on his way in an ambulance. My husband and I drove in silence, but pangs of panic stabbed at our hearts over and over again, cramping our thoughts into fragments of more panic. We arrived in the back of the Ventura County Hospital, where we met the ambulance and they were wheeling Israel into a scanning machine room. Israel lay motionless, as his young tan body seemed lifeless.

"Israel! Israel! Israel!" I called to him! I stroked his head and chest, but there was no answer. I didn't understand what it meant. No response! Was he alive? Was he breathing? I heard nothing after that! Shock shook my brain like a hurricane, and I couldn't seem to hear the conversations that the medical attendants were having with me and my husband.

On August 1992, my family began a journey into the world of head injury, a three-month coma, and three-year trial. This became a nightmare I never knew could exist in this life. We witnessed the struggle between spirit and body, God and medical technology, death and life, faith and fear, demons and angels, and ordinary people who loved their son and could not and would not limit themselves to being powerless. A family that believed the body has a spirit given by God that precedes the brain, and when in the hands of God, has precedence over the brain in the realm where we believed God rules.

I followed my husband into the elevator, aching with fear and assuming I must be hallucinating, as the numerous men in white coats ignored me. We arrived at the top floor where the I.C.U. awaited us and my son Israel. It seemed like a place in between heaven and hell where families began tense struggles to separate reality from medical diagnosis. As most families seemed to lose the battle, I studied them, evening after evening, accepting the doctor's word. I comforted them in my heart, but denied myself the uncomfortable feeling of the collective bond that lived in the waiting room offering no hope to the families or the member who laid behind closed doors called I.C.U.

The second evening after we arrived, I waited in the room outside of the I.C.U. and my mind drifted into the memory of the dream I had the previous month. Israel was in an icy ocean, and his head kept going under the water and I was nearby, struggling to swim to him. I continued to stay above water as Israel seemed to be losing his struggle against the raging waters around him. Now I nudged my husband, but his anxiety distanced me, so I continued in the memory and the dream held fast as I remembered the craft that came out of nowhere, and the person in white who piloted the craft and helped me pull Israel on board and we were whisked away to safety.

I scrambled up to ring the bell again, demanding they let me in to see my son. He was lying quiet and no movement was apparent. My husband stepped outside to speak with the doctors concerning his condition, which came with all the terminology of cranial pressure, brain damage, vegetative state, and later a fungal infection that lived in his entire system and would kill him. We stayed until exhaustion overtook our minds and bodies, and drove home in silence, but we seemed to be in a desert, going nowhere.

Awake all night going over the medical diagnosis, I found the tears just swallowed up the answers of hope I sought for. After scrambling to reach the police station for some answers, we waited to speak to the police officer who interviewed the two boys who survived the accident before our daily work schedule would demand our attention. We remained calm as we listened.

The story told by the front-seat passengers was that Israel had been ejected thirty feet into the air out of the back of a small pickup truck, as the truck swirled around and rolled twice after it dumped him into the drainage ditch, where he ended face-up in a pool water. The ambulance arrived after a call was made by a driver traveling on the same road opposite the direction of the traveling pickup, and at the distance of a football field when the accident happened. The driver said he saw Israel ejected out of the pickup as it was beginning to turn over.

The police had questioned the boys for several hours after the accident and found no use drugs or alcohol and no skid marks denoting unlawful speed. "It wasn't the fault of the boys!" stated the officer, almost as if he was complaining to me that I was presuming judgment. He seemed defensive and protective of the boys, and that left me feeling confused. Besides, I wasn't looking for harm to another young person. I just wanted to know the truth, but I noted that the officer never asked me how my son or my family was doing. His was a different motive and a different perspective, too.

I was a mom with a family in need of answers that would haunt me for the rest of my life. I spent hours comforting friends, as well as explaining the details to the families of the two boys who had crawled out of the cab safely.

George was at my side, but silence was spreading like a cancer, for our comfort was miles away, and our relatives lived in the Midwest and on the East Coast. Our daughter, Michelle, continued to go to school and was nominated for Homecoming Queen during our trauma, but the timing for her was bad. Fears and faith collided as we wrestled in our love for Israel. I heard that voice inside me asking: "Did not Jacob wrestle with the angel and his name was changed to Israel? Because he persisted to get God's blessing, he did! And God's blessing was upon him."

I began to realize the battle was a spiritual one as well as emotional and I would have to choose which would rule.

5

That evening, the neurologist pulled my husband to the hallway outside the I.C.U. My husband shared the conversation with me later. They were asking for a decision on life-support removal, Israel was a vegetable; brain dead in a coma.

2

County Hospital

Standing in the I.C.U. of the county hospital, we waited for the doctors and the explanation they gave with grave faces getting worse with each new complication. Cranial pressure had subsided slightly with the use of brand-name barbiturates after the generic brand failed, and during the weekend, they ran out of his drugs and the cranial pressure returned.

A trache was in his throat to help him breathe and August was the month when we put him on total life-support. I received a call from the chiropractor, Dr Johnson, who had seen the kids on a free exam and he offered to spend every morning doing hand massage above the brain stem to improve the flow of oxygen. The hospital disapproved and argued the doctor had no credentials, according to the head nurse.

After rounds of confrontation, they finally allowed him to continue. He was an angel, and gave us hope. "Excuse me?" my daughter said as she approached the nurse. "Why is my brother's left hand so cold?" I watched as they reassured her that it was nothing to be alarmed about, as they had told my husband in his earlier questioning. Besides, how much more danger could he be in? He was comatose and in a vegetative state.

A call was made to me from the intern assigned to Israel's case asking questions about the cause of the accident. He wanted an investigation done by the police! "Why?" I questioned him. He stated he had been in the medical field a long time and if Israel had been in this type of an accident, there would be broken bones. What did he mean? They had the ambulance and the police records. I called the head neurosurgeon to discuss this request and he started to ignore it and said it was some misunderstanding. I explained to him again that even the doctor thought there may have been foul play or that someone dumped him in the ditch. The inquisitive doctor was later removed from the case after that phone call. The new doctor from Virginia was an intern who seemed sensitive, even though he was constantly badgered by my stream of questions and challenging behavior. The infectious disease doctor called around fourteen days into Israel's coma to get my signature for insulin, as Israel wasn't producing any on his own. A new issue plagued us: they wanted to amputate Israel's left arm. It was full of gangrene and needed to be removed up to the elbow or above.

He had contracted a rare fungal infection, generally found in diabetics. The fungus was on his knee and was also considered to be systematic by the staff. We then learned of a broken collarbone on the left side which was recorded in the nurses' notes! A meeting was called to convince us to remove the left arm, even though his body was infected with the fungus and it would eventually cause death. We tried hard to avoid the decision as if a death sentence had been unjustly imposed on Israel. A storm of tears and questions drove our adrenalin to the heights.

I rebelled against this diagnosis like it was a demon. I phoned every local alternative medicine doctor available and requested they phone the intern who held Israel on this rope of life and death. I finally accepted the counsel that in a hospital setting surrounded by doctors who didn't practice alternative methods, amputation was inevitable. The days passed quickly. We were alone with our faith in God, sharing with each person who cared for Israel in any way. Israel opened one eye, and seemed to have movement in his hand. We were told it was reflexes, and he was still in a coma and in a vegetative state.

A small ring that had been placed on Israel's left hand, was found missing after the amputation. It said: "I love Jesus," and it was our bond when we left the hospital reminding each shift he was in God's hands, who was greater than death. I put a note on the billboard in his room demanding the return of the ring. We arrived the next evening, and they were suctioning Israel to clear his lungs, and I always remained out of the room when it was done. The medical procedure was not known to me before Israel's accident, and to me, the procedure reminded me of death.

I stormed out of the room to the front desk. "What medication did you give my son?" The nurse looked at me in surprise and pulled the chart to answer my question. My intuition was keen as if I had a sixth sense. "The doctor gave him an antipsychotic drug for muscle spasms," she said. "You will not give him any drugs without our permission!" I ranted and raved until the doctor arrived. We left the hospital late, and you could read the pain in our faces, like we'd been in a war-torn country for too long. On the way home, my husband comforted us by reminding me that God was able to overcome even the doctor's mistakes.

My son's face and silence overcame me, and that evening I sat at the kitchen table and wrote my son a poem.

Silence

The chair in the corner,
speaks to you of emptiness,
like the vase nearby that sits to rest.

Your thoughts running through,
the caverns of time,
are all empty too,
and locked in your mind.

Like tears in a bottle,
gone out to sea,
with a promise to return free.

Books on the shelf,
standing so still,
whisper secretly
against your will.

You jumble with the ring,
that's on your hand,
placed by someone
who believes you can,

Yet the objects are still,
with no freedom to move,
and it makes me wonder.
With a magic wand,
if they could.

But your silence remains,
until the time,
when God will move and awake you inside,
and all the objects,
within your reach
will move in your mind,
and begin to speak.

And then you'll know,
you'll know for sure,
your silence has been heard.

We were weary with anger and fatigue as we prayed for strength for guidance in medical decisions that would continue to halt the use of drugs and surgery, and convince the medical staff that we were believing in God for our son's recovery. We prayed, we talked about our prayers, we talked about praying, and read everything we could about comas, recovery, and most all, building the immune system.

A friend of Israel's called me in September, almost a month after his accident He had been on the swim team with my son, and wanted to confirm to me that my son did hear me when I spoke to him. I was at a low ebb, as the staff didn't believe that he could hear and they also spoke in his room near his bed that he would die. I rushed to the hospital that night and continued to sing, and talk to my son, playing tapes and organizing everyone he knew to keep talking to him. I scolded the nurses and doctors for their speaking in his room about death.

My sister in Minnesota called that evening and began to remind me of so many things I had forgotten in nutrition. I purchased a high strain of acidophilus at the health store and requested the doctor to write a prescription for the nurses to place it in the bag three times a day.

We had already upped his vitamin C and zinc through his doctor, and were using homeopathic pills under his tongue for additional nutrition. God used this nutrition three times a day to bring Israel's compromised immune system, fungal infection, and pneumonia under control. I started gaining a sense of progress when I was called into a quiet room with the intern and a house psychologist. "Israel's going to die!" the intern said. I could see the tears streaming down his face, as he spoke. "What do you want the doctor to do?" the house psychologist inquired. "Nobody can stop this merry-go-round; it happens at every hospital when you have a tragedy like your son," he said.

In the back of my mind, I remembered the nurse speaking about the possibility of another amputation of my son's knee, and speaking over both of them, I said, "I don't believe in your fungal infection and if you can't believe on your own that my son will live, then believe with me." I felt for the doctor, but I was not moved. I will always remember him. I told him, "I do believe you care and believe you will be a good doctor some day." I had to leave, for I had more important voices to listen to. I stopped at my son's bed again and noticed his left eye opened again and I sat quietly and prayed, and watched over him with the Lord.

It was a Wednesday and I arrived at the hospital at noon and found that friends had come and gone. Remembering them as they hurdled in the waiting room the first evening, frightened and confused, now leaving with a new witness of memories that they were planning on placing behind them. Jenell was in the room, kissing and talking to Israel as he laid there still and silent. I glanced at their photographs of the graduation dance placed on the billboard and thought about young people, and how they would find solace in life through so much pain. "Izz," she said, "I love you! Give me a kiss!" Jenell and I hugged, and her energy was good.

I drove home alone that day, and suddenly a bicyclist pulled into the road, as I screeched on my brakes. An officer, who had been two cars behind me, flashed his blue light and pulled the boy into the parking lot to give him a ticket. I continued home, relieved that I had avoided getting into an accident.

As I arrived home, my daughter Michelle was sitting at the table. She stood up and said, "Hi, Mom, how is Israel?" We talked, embraced, and comforted each other. After she left, I rummaged through her school things that were on the table, and opened a crumpled paper that read:

Your Face

Visions of your smile
wander throughout my head
thinking of words that might be said
to describe the glowing twinkle
within your eyes
with no barrier present to represent disguise

The distinct lines
in your curvaceous jaw
remind me of a perfect form
of a seesaw.

The wrinkles in your forehead
there but faint
show wisdom
with strokes of invisible paint
your eyelashes
make me think clearly
of a fun slide
of a special friend
in whom you'd confide

Even though these things may change
due to time
to me
your beautiful face will always shine.

The following day, I further agitated the intern and
asked that the trache in Israel's throat be removed, after Israel was moved out of I.C.U. and into the telemetry unit.
While Israel was in a coma, he had developed pneumonia
three times due to the trache in his throat, but now he was
breathing on his own without any oxygen machine giving
him assistance. They now placed a temporary button in his
throat. It was the end of October 1992, and after months
spent in applying music for therapy. Headphones were used
as well as familiar tapes, and it was then that Israel began to
snap his fingers to the oldies on the radio. He also faced surgery to place the tube in his stomach for permanent feeding,
and drugs were brought down to a minimum.

Although the intern stated it was an easy surgery, re-
siduals kept coming back out of the tube, showing it wasn't
feeding him. They put him back on I.V. tubes to feed him,
with all the complications and negative implications that it
brought with it. We went home that night feeling defeated,
but when we awoke, we shared the dreams that God gave

us. In my dream I entered the hospital where the nurse had placed a mattress over him like a cover. I then hurried and stole Israel out of the hospital, and took him home. When he arrived home, he sat up on his bed and began to speak to me just like a movie picture. It seemed real.

I was so excited I wanted to shout! "He's alive and well and he can talk." Before I could share my dream, George calmly told me he saw Israel walking in his dream, and "He will walk," he said. I was excited with our hope, but somehow we thought we were being delusional. We didn't care; we followed our dreams and bonded in believing what implications they had. The removal of the trache comforted me as I had a difficult time with the suctioning process. It seemed cruel as I watched my son gag and struggle so hard to live and it pulled his body so recklessly. I developed a deep dislike for the life-support system. The nurses watched out of the corner of their work station as we tried to help his immune system with echinacea, goldenseal, and vitamin C, fighting against drugs in his body and the tubes that were attached to his body.

The coffee overflowed from my cup, and I heard the manager ordering food for me, as she had done since the employees at Bob's Big Boy restaurant heard of Israel's coma. Envisioning my son behind the counter where he would have been working this time of day, I could see him laughing and mingling with the locals as the older folks would kid him about girls and teenage talk.

I unencumbered myself of sadness with Tammy, who hired my son and was very fond of him, becoming a mentor and friend for life. All of the staff visited him frequently and all of them prayed daily, some, I felt, maybe had not ever really prayed that hard for anyone before. Tammy somehow healed me with her smile and compassion, and I felt stronger than when I first arrived. It felt strange, like angels watching over you, common people, and the power of love. I wrote songs about this type of love when I was in the ministry, down to earth love, and I searched for it in churches amongst professing Christians and it was simply abundant among these friends of my son. I took as much as I could and rejoiced for love's sake, and still remember the tears and prayers.

I wished everyone in life could be blessed in their trials. I rejoiced for my son, that he was so loved at this time in his struggle to live. Watching the I.V. tubes dripping from the bag and into my son's right arm, we observed the danger of infection, after amputation of the left arm, as well as the weight he had continually lost. How could he survive? I ordered the doctor on call to the room whenever we arrived, and it was always someone new, and sometimes no one arrived. And the nurses answered the questions with assumptions. The answer to the feeding problem was that the doctor went on vacation and he was the only surgeon who could try to place the tubes in the small intestine.

Energy sucked life from my family like a leech drawing blood. Were they letting him die? The doctor's statement rang in my memory, *Israel is going to die from the fungus in his system*. I scrambled to the icebox behind the nurses' station to be sure they were using the acidophilus the doctor agreed to keep him on. Then I prayed and went home to rest. The next evening as my husband stood on the other side of the bed as a caregiver positioning pillows, cleaning his bowels, and wiping his forehead; the daily ritual in his dance of mourning and love, we began to pray together. Within minutes of praying and laying our hands on our son's forehead, George said, "I felt that healing!" I experienced a strange warm feeling passing from my arm into his body, similar to many times when I had prayed in the ministry for others. I looked and viewed Israel's face tenderly as if he would awake like a newborn and our nightmare would end. He lay quietly, but we held on to the belief that God had touched him and would keep healing him, and we would wait. My son remained in a semi-coma.

Nearly three months had passed since the accident and my daughter arrived at the hospital after getting out of school. "How are you doing, Izzy?" she said. "I love you!" She smiled at him and jested like a sister or girlfriend ignoring her pain, but always appearing more realistic than her father or me. She had a ritual with her brother, a lot like her father's, she moved his legs, and made him seem more comfortable.

She smiled at me, taking my pain upon herself in a gentle way. Suddenly we were abruptly disturbed by my son's upper body pulling itself up and forward. "I'm f—ing mad!" he whispered. The anger was ignored, as his voice was music to our ears. We jumped up and down and embraced. "Mom! Did you hear that!" I nodded and we embraced again. I cried out, "I did! Thank God I did!" The staff gathered around noon in front of my son's room and we stood amongst them, while congratulations were being spoken to other medical personnel who had cared for Israel in the I.C.U. and in the telemetry unit. My son was being transferred into the C West unit after the doctor had arrived back from vacation and placed a new feeding tube into the small intestine. It took nearly three days before it started working right and was feeding him the nutrition he needed to survive, as he had lost a great deal of weight.

"I would like to congratulate the staff for their teamwork and professionalism!" The doctor proceeded to say. I spoke out of turn like usual since the accident. "I believe the glory goes to God!" I felt the words pass by each staff member in a different way. But the head doctor and speaker seem to choke on the statement and as he glared at me, the anger seemed to be foaming in his mouth. A smile from the female nurse seemed to signal a dispersement of the crowd. October was coming to an end, and we were entering a new phase of our son's recovery.

As they dispersed, no one spoke to Israel to somehow acknowledge that he could hear them. My son was then transferred to the unit down the hall where he would spend another month, preparing him for a rehab facility. By that afternoon my son's ring was mysteriously returned, and placed on the billboard where his personal photos were. I placed it back on his right middle finger, while a nurse broke the tension with her statement: "Someone else must have needed it worse than Israel."

By this time I had accomplished getting him the minimum amount of medications and was feeling encouraged. I checked at the front desk, confronting the new staff that would care for him, and introduced myself. "How is my son today?" I asked the blond nurse who finally took notice of me standing at the counter. "You know, Mrs. Echevarria," she answered, "hospitals are full of kids like your son! And, all they do is sit and drool all day. There are hundreds of them in institutions and nursing homes. You need to accept that!" I had heard this kind of opinion over and over again, and I was used to it. The nurse in I.C.U. said he would die or be a vegetable, and she still sits on the back burner in my memory. Thanksgiving holiday had arrived and we reluctantly left the hospital to find a place to eat. The food had arrived, but I felt salty tears running down my face.

"What's the matter!" my daughter said. "I can't wait to see Israel eat and eat and eat." I said. My husband smiled and said, "He will!" And we all smiled in our gratefulness for God's healing. Anxious to transfer my son to a new facility, I had a new challenge ahead of me. Israel's sodium levels were so low the county hospital had to keep him two more weeks. The HMO caseworker continued to prepare for placing him three hours away, while I begged for a closer facility. And there were other sales people from different local facilities wanting him. Only then did I understand more of the insurance politics and what cutting costs was all about.

After all, my son was first in St. John's Hospital and then transferred to the county hospital for unknown reasons. We questioned our private insurance status and that didn't seem to give us rights. Vulnerable to all the pressure, we would soon face a six-hour drive daily after work to care for Israel and to return to work daily. Focusing on our son and his recovery blinded us to our rights and we were fighting so hard already. They improved his sodium levels and he made the trip to rehab three hours away. This became the most stressful part of his recovery.

3

Rehabilitation

The coast along Highway 1 was blowing with Santa Anna winds, as our Honda rocked back and forth. It was Christmas and we were anxious to arrive at the Rehab hospital. The car began to slow down and stall, leaving us on a dark road. We let it roll into a station about a mile beyond. It was a miracle there was help so close by from a gas station on the coast where the ocean and the stretch of land took you winding into nowhere near help. The clutch had gone out and we had to leave the vehicle there. My daughter and our friend Carol bravely fought the winds and brought the other Honda, which was not in any better condition. "Mom! I could barely see, I was so scared, the winds were blowing me all over the road." We were all concerned and scared; we knew the vehicles we had could not take a daily six-hour drive, but we finally got on our way. We climbed in the small Honda and kissed our daughter good-bye as soon as her ride home arrived.

We would stay the weekend and were encouraged that we would find new help for his recovery there. They were examining him when we arrived, and we watched as the nurses gazed at the huge bedsores on his buttocks and feet, and commented on his weight of 80 pounds. But as the days followed, so did spiking fevers, ice beds, screaming pain as they dressed these open sores three times a day. Israel was still semi-comatose and very frightened.

They tied his only arm to the bed, as he rocked and rocked and rocked off his right hip, he pulled all the feeding tubes out of his stomach and the catheter off his private parts. Sometimes three people had to hold him down. He was verbally abusive and angry, his pain seemed unbearable. "What's happening, Dad?" he whispered. His eyes were wide and glazed, but he knew his family well. His agitation was constant and verbal as he exercised his need for help. I wandered through the coma ward and studied different coma patients, those who had some recovery, and others on life-support. We immediately took responsibility to clean, bathe, and change his clothes, while working in dressing the bedsores. I handed the nutritionist the book on nutritional healing and negotiated with her to read it in three days, and cooperate in supplementing his diet with liquid amino acids, c10 enzyme, acidophilus, ginkgo biloba, chlorophyll, and comfrey. I was grateful for the follow-up. Pain was a subject I constantly studied and I only heard later that head injury patients have low tolerance for pain. I called daily and I could hear him screaming through the hall for help, and I felt there was something wrong causing him pain.

The staff accepted it as a head injury behavior, but I knew that his painful rocking back and forth on the bed was not normal pain behavior. I received a call from the speech therapist the following day after the weekend ended. I inquired about his speech. Her response was that he probably would not ever speak other than a whisper. Her assurance and calmness filled my body with tension, "Oh! He'll talk," I said, "You bet he will!" Silence filled the phone and the weeks passed and the nurses followed the nutritional regime that I requested. He was talking as clearly as could be. No seizures, no stuttering, and a small amount of slurring. The nurses would go to his room in amazement and ask if he remembered their names. He always said "Miss Beautiful" to each and every one. I thanked God he could at least protect himself from things that he might encounter when we were not there by his side. Five days a week after work, we made the long journey to visit our son, to and from the rehabilitation center, except on weekends when we stayed overnight.

"Hi! I am Danny!" I heard as I rushed to the room late on a Thursday night. "Hi!" I said, wondering who he was and why he seemed so friendly and supportive. I became friends with him and learned to identify with his tragedy. His wife was on full life-support as she had had surgery on her brain for migraine headaches. The surgery was not successful, but he was there every evening by her side.

He brushed her hair and rubbed her feet, and completely adored her. She was motionless. I will always remember him and my memory of his love unseen by the human eye. I entered the room and held her hand and I told her how much Danny was in love with her. Her fingers mingled with mine, and for a moment, our spirits touched. Danny also watched over Israel when we arrived late, he was an angel. His wife never recovered, and he took her home with a full-time nurse, and cameras watched her day and night. He became disturbed one day when they shut the door to Israel's room, so he went to the head staff and threatened to report them if it happened again. Israel fell off the bed a week later. We suggested he be put on a flat sponge mattress on the floor, after they had already experimented with a circus bed, something like a canopy, confining his sight and mobility.

With the flat bed in use, we were able to spend time near him, nurturing him, working with his memory, and bringing him back to feeling safe again. We had already been feeding him organic baby food for three weeks, before they introduced solid food. Later, we requested they remove the feeding tubes from his stomach, meeting great opposition from them, but soon they removed them. Encouraging them to remove the catheter and teaching him to use the urinal was another slow process. We started doing it and my son picked it up quickly. Pain haunted us constantly and as we left in the evenings, we took his pain with us, talking incessantly and searching for answers. I drove down the following day during a terrible rainstorm, and when I arrived, I found my son in the therapy room. The nurse had placed him on his stomach over a ball.

Israel was swearing at her and trying to flip her over his side with his right hand and arm. I felt sickened by the sight and demanded that all therapy be stopped until further Xrays for pain were done. She dismissed us both with the statement: "I don't think Israel likes me!" I mumbled under my breath, "I didn't think so either." The Xray was scheduled and a hairline fracture was found on the right hip, with seriously brittle bones. My mind wandered back to the first doctor at the county hospital who questioned the notes that didn't have any documents on broken bones, and was later removed from our son's medical care. I became busy with my job and the other aspects of my son's injury. During the first month of the coma, I was approached by clients interested in my son's tragedy. I was referred to a personal injury law firm by them and they encouraged me on Israel's recovery. The attorneys I contacted immediately went to the site of the accident and started video-taping my son at the hospital. This was the beginning of a three-year litigation and three months trial involving the pickup truck called a Subaru Brat (a very small pickup with plastic seats in the back, sold as fun-in-the-sun in their advertisements).

March was arriving and progress was more and more difficult as we drove three hours to the rehab hospital, and three hours home each weekday after work and weekends. It was not taking the anxiety out of the negative feeling we had about the insurance companies and their attempts to direct him into one of their rehab homes. The staff kept encouraging us to visit group homes and to consider placing our son under our insurance, in a facility near them, or the one they promised would be opened near our home. The first week in March, we followed the winding hills to pay a visit to the rehab home they thought we would like the best. An attractive tall redheaded female answered the door and invited us into the facility where many young people were still on life-support and lay quietly in their beds at 12:00 noon.

I questioned the whereabouts of the parents. Why were the drapes still closed, and why were these young people still on breathing machines? She said: "The parents feel they are safe here and trust us, and the insurance companies pay for their care." I felt the violation for each one of them, for there was no family there, only routine! I cried for those head injury victims without families. I tugged at my husband's coat and tried to be as polite as I could and believed there must be a special situation in each life. I just didn't get it and didn't want to be part of it. My chest ached and we hurried back to see my son alive and well as he could be, and I praised the Lord.

I assured the staff this was not for Israel and I would be removing him as soon as possible, giving March 8 as the date of his release. They tried to object on home-care issues, elevator problems, etc. I reminded them that my son had fallen out of bed with brittle bones in their facility. They let it go! The ambulance arrived on time and my son recognized his neighborhood. "It even smells like home," he said, as they lifted him two flights and then he was left sitting in the living room. The ambulance driver stood silent and then I began to sob. "Israel! Finally you are home, this is what I've waited for so long." He reached down and stroked my face. "Don't cry Mom!" And we hugged each other. The mail arrived late that day, and we were comforted by a letter from my sister, Julie

Sande, and enclosed she attached this poem, which she wrote:

Trials

God may take us to the valley
but he'll never leave us there,
his love will come to lift us,
from the trial that we bear.

He may lead us to the desert,
but He will come again
to give us healing from our sorrow.
and cleansing from our sin.

He may send us thru the fire,
but He will be there too,
to shield us from destruction,
and bring us safely thru.

And should He let the waters rise,
to cover o'er our soul,
He'll return again to part them,
He'll return to make us whole.

Israel (football) 7th grade.

Israel at Jenell's graduation prom (June 1992).

A Subaru Brat truck with a passenger seat.

August 1992, Subaru in ditch after ejecting Israel.

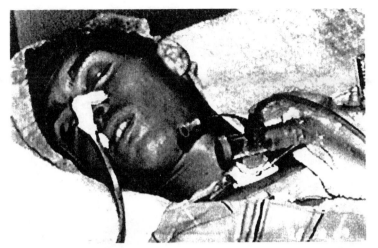

August 1992, comatose, County Hospital.

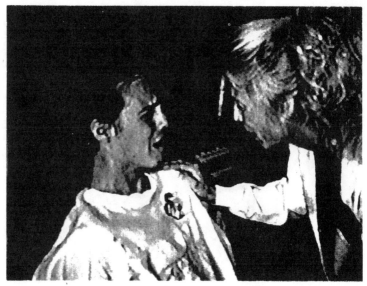

First day at home (March 1993). "Mom, don't cry."

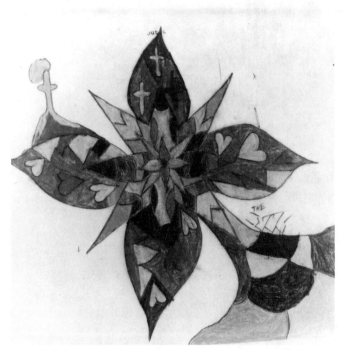

Artwork done as soon as Israel returned home (by Israel).

Israel swims laps daily.

Israel determined to walk.

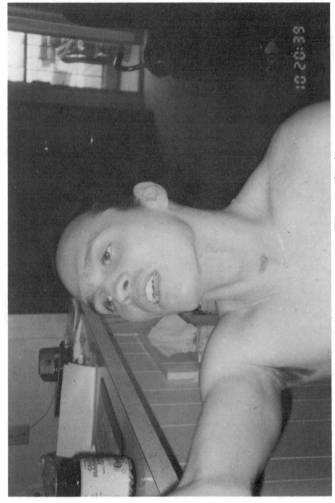

Israel singing, now attending music classes.

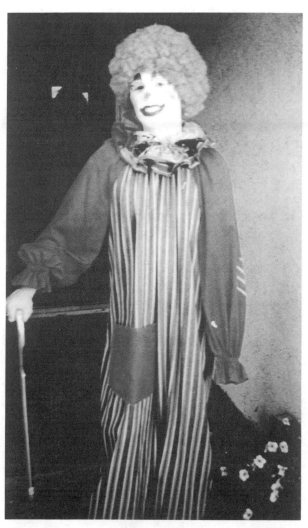

Israel (as a clown) donating time to Easter Seals.

Family after a swim in the pool. George, Patricia, Michelle, and Israel.

4

Home

I couldn't believe we were doing all the things they said we would never do. We purchased a large plastic raft boat for bathing and kept Israel on the sponge mat we purchased for sleeping. We then entered the local community health facility, looking for assistance on the hip fracture and for pain problems. They did bone scans and Xrays and couldn't find any hip fracture. We continued stretching him and eventually rejected the drugs given for the heretropic bone wrapped around his right hip. They had put him in deep depression and we could not endure depression along with all his losses. He began wearing glasses as he had some sight problems, and had his wisdom teeth removed. My son acquired his high school diploma after some objection from the school. Before his accident he had two weeks to finish. Vomiting was a problem in the early months, but his stomach was healing from all the drugs and the surgery on his left arm. My son took charge of healing himself and he detoxed his system faithfully with water daily. Israel's grief and anger were real, and it took many family discussions on love to begin to heal and remove any death wish that might be in his heart. We fit a prosthesis for his left arm with hours of therapy, all of which he rejected. So we focused on getting him to walk and loving one another.

The accident occurred in August 1992, we were now in 1994, and this was our second Christmas at home with our son. Many friends came, as Israel was someone everybody knew in school. I was grateful to God he had the same personality, and his long-term memory seemed nearly restored. He remembered people who didn't recognize him, but he always had problems with names. We spent a year with the chiropractor, and we continued to use nutrition as our foundation for building his health. Treating disease is an unnatural thing, and rebuilding the body so it can do its job was a testimony for our son and was much of his recovery. In a Turkish study of 20 patients with severe head injuries who took Dimethylsulfoxide (DMSO) within a few hours after receiving the injury up until six hours afterward, pressure in the brain was relieved at a 75 percent rate: fourteen lived and only one sustained nerve damage. By contrast, of the 30,000 people who suffer head trauma every year, 66 percent die in the emergency room, 2,500 remain comatose, and of the 7,500 who survive, most had a high degree of brain damage. Israel falls into the percentage of miracles.

It starts with a dream you believe in and faith in God and miracles do come true. In April all blood tests were normal, no fungi was found, his left-side amputation healed fully, and we saved his leg from amputation.

No CAT scan records of his entire body were ever recovered from the nurses' notes according to the attorneys. We requested an investigation into the notes by an M.D. attorney and no notes were found on hand. We brought this to the attention of the nurses. As the attorneys pursued litigation against the automobile company a silence reigned over the medical community that had first treated my son, and phone calls were not being returned, as solutions to pain were drug-related and for mental health purposes rejected by us. We added to his nutritional program, as he endured the unbearable pain in his right hip. We flew our son to the University of Minnesota Medical Center for a second opinion, as we were unable to get a confirmation of a right hip fracture.

It was finally noted in the Xray that he either had a malunion or non-union right hip fracture. The doctor attending us asked if anyone ever told him that my son would have ambulation. I said, "Only me!" He looked at me grimly and wished me luck. My son was agitated at the negative response from the doctor, and the trip home to California was filled with a longing for renewed hope. We enrolled Israel in a local college while his litigation was pending, for it had been set back on the court calendar due to overcrowding by the "three strikes and you're out law." He tried art classes for the physically impaired, but pain from his right hip kept him from concentration. Then the attorneys on both sides began sending us to medical doctors and neuro-psychiatrists for purposes of the trial. The humiliation was difficult for the entire family.

Our attorneys were constantly looking for deficits or ignoring the seriousness of our son's recovery for the proposed purpose of gaining monetary lifetime care for him, and the opposing attorney was looking for competence. George and I cringed at the cooperation necessary for the stream of questions that would be proposed for the battle ahead in the personal injury trial. We carefully mentored our son and educated him on the purpose of the trial versus our goals of recovery. We were angry, for we wanted to get our son into surgery and walking; instead it would be three months of viewing his deficits daily. It became especially painful to me, because I objected to any thoughts of placing my son in any facility that would take away his independence and chance for recovery. This trial changed our lives in different ways, and left us questioning the legal system.

July, September, and October were filled with newspaper publicity and so we continued to cooperate and wait on the surgery, and wonder where it would take our family emotionally. With direction from the Lord, we were able to move into a new apartment, with a jacuzzi and a pool, and to put our hearts and minds together for our son for further recovery. Art work became a therapy for him, and he began

41

his own flower creations, flowers within flowers and perfecting the coloring in each petal. It reminded me of the memory and it was like a new sunlight watching his talents given by God, finding their way through his brain, and out of his spirit. His gift back to life.

5

The Trial

The lawsuit was filed in July of 1992, and the trial would take eleven weeks and end on September 21, 1995. We sat quietly in back of the courtroom, and I asked God for discernment. I watched my attorney as he wrestled with his small word processor sitting a few rows in front of me, and the opposing attorney paced back and forth in the aisle with her hands wringing behind her back, her face red with real intention, and her expression cold. Early on I heard my attorney mention to her that this case was about the jury, but she jerked her head and said, "The judge," with no additional sentence to add it to. I assumed they were debating who would have greater power over the decision of liability, the judge or jury.

Our attorneys were suing Fuji Inc. and Subaru automobile makers for having no safety testing and selling a small pickup truck with plastic seats placed in the open bed of the vehicle in the back for young people to ride in, and the City of Oxnard, in Ventura County, California, for having a dangerous road, with no shoulder and lighting. This road was frequently used by young people, who came directly from high school. The Subaru Brat vehicle was featured in a fun-in-the-sun advertisement, and young people were targeted for sales. We had been through the gruelling depositions that tested our character and took away our time from the miracle of our son and the healing we needed.

The opposing attorneys disappeared into the judge's quarters and left our attorney sitting there ignoring the silence in the room. I thought about the conversation they had before they disappeared and wondered in what political way it was really applicable.

The following week was jury picking and I was counseled on how to dress and project myself. I had minor difficulties with it other than that I worked full time, and *I* felt on trial for something! I guess sometimes we all have a sense of being part of the problem and not the solution. The jury picking was tedious and just before it seemed that they had accomplished it, a young girl stood up and spoke in a very emotional voice: "I could never be on this jury, because I rode in the of back of a Brat pickup and I was scared to death! I think they are dangerous!" And she made her way down the aisle after the judge dismissed her. They continued and the trial finally got on its way. I thought about Israel and knew that he would hear issues of incompetence and negative feedback from the opposing party; even his own attorney would be presenting him to the jury in the worst way possible. I constantly argued with our attorney on these issues, only to find myself in between the devil and the deep blue sea. It broke my heart and left me suspicious of the purpose of the justice system. They put each juror through rigorous questioning on prejudices and any reasons past or present why each should not be a juror on this personal injury trial.

Jury picking ended when both attorneys were satisfied. Both sides had a jury consultant who was hired for expertise in picking the jury. Each phase brought specialists for both sides who testified on roll-over crashworthiness and finally malice for punitive damages. Israel's attorneys focused on the fact that Subaru sold the truck as a passenger vehicle only in the United States, placing the plastic seats in the back for a customs and tariff scam. During the graphic videos of Israel's recovery, which showed him on life-support, one of the younger female jurors had fainted in the hall during a break from the trial, and all of the people in the courtroom rushed out to the hall to see what the commotion was about. The medical doctor who had treated him and was testifying on Israel's behalf hovered over her and assisted until she was fine. The opposing side rushed back into the courtroom to urge the judge to call a mistrial. The request was denied. The trial continued as more specialists took the stand and doctors for both sides gave statements on the injuries sustained by Israel and his loss for a lifetime. The judge was very polished, always smiling, and continually cared for the jurors like his sons and daughters.

Laughter filled the courtroom daily. After a break in between periods, the attorneys approached the bench. Jokes and compliments to individual jurors seemed to stroke them and they did seem like one big happy family. The first phase established liability, and the newspaper later recorded a juror stating, "If you place seats in the bed of a truck, [the passenger's] head should not be above the roof," (*Ventura County News,* Sept. 21, 1995), and that alone was a defect. During the second phase, a new lead juror was chosen, and they proceeded with the punitive damages, which were to show malice in the trial, as the fact that no previous safety testing had been done was brought up on the trial. The punitive damages were not proven as malice was not perceived. The courtroom became quiet as the end to a three-month trial brought its verdict to Israel and our family. The contradiction that the vehicle was defective and yet there was no malice became the settlement emotionally, and somehow it never seemed to be about the incredible tragedy that will take a family and an eighteen-year-old a lifetime to accept. The closing statements from our attorney were strong and powerful. They came from inside of him as if he were personally attached to the case and to Israel.

The city attorney and the attorneys for the Fuji and Subaru Corporation stood together throughout the trial. We stood against them as two against one. The female attorney

45

frequently studied our family as she would turn her head and look solemnly at us, and me in particular. I whispered to my husband concerning their witnesses, and later was reprimanded by my attorney that she complained to the judge concerning our motions. The city attorney left a scar on the family when speaking to the jury he compared Israel to Humpty Dumpty who fell off a wall and all the kings' horses and all the kings' men couldn't put him back together again.

As he entertained the jury with his riddle, I watched my son and hoped that he would forgive this little sarcastic man. After the punitive verdict was announced, the lead juror immediately left his seated position and quickly passed in front of the table that Israel was seated at, and arrived at the table of the opposing attorneys. He extended his hand to shake the attorneys hand, as others mumbled that there must have been some kind of mistake and there would be an appeal for sure. The memory of the smiling juror shaking hands in victory mocked my values of compassion, and changed my concept of juries and the justice system. The newspaper cameras gathered around as they seemed disappointed and asked about an appeal. I wanted to go home and thank God it was over, but it wasn't that easy for our attorneys.

6

Settlement

Streams of phone calls went back and forth, as the dust settled and an appeal was in the minds of our attorneys. We had no energy or time for an appeal, which would set back our dream of surgery, which had already waited the three-year span of time it took to get into trial. Our attorneys were distraught at the loss of punitive damages, and our attorney approached a juror. "Don't you know what you did?" he scolded them. "You left this kid nothing!" The conversation got back to the judge and he made a phone call chastising our attorney.

The liability was $1.5 million and the attorneys' fees were more than that. Adding to the politics, a court-appointed attorney was hired, paid by the settlement, ordered by the judge to investigate attorney fees. I made daily calls to the law office. We would not appeal, leaving Israel on another merry-go-round with the politics of the law. This time the stress was coming from our own attorneys again. When I was phoned by my attorney, all my preconceptions and every trusting thought left me tired and unprepared to announce to Israel and my family the outcome. The attorneys' fees were more than the settlement. We would be urged to accept a few hundred thousand as charity. God would have to harness our outrage, to have overcome our fears and supply our needs. I must have called nine attorneys, trying to understand who was responsible to educate the jury on attorneys' fees. It was nearly a year later when I was finally told by an attorney that there was a special form to be filed before a trial, stating that if there was a settlement won, all attorneys' fees not be paid from the settlement to the client.

I wish I could warn every honest human being I could find. Later I realized there were many of us out there and there were more things in the justice system that would never work for ordinary people.

7

Conservatorship

A conservatorship was court-ordered by the judge with no communication with the family, to be controlled by local and court-appointed attorneys to oversee the attorneys who would oversee the mounds and mounds of receipts and faxes for approval of all and anything needed by Israel. All were paid well out of the small settlement the personal injury attorneys submitted as charity. Everyone got paid and I had to approach the courts for waiving the bond to be allowed to continue in my quest for recovery for my son. I finally took charge of the accounting and submitted monthly reports to the court-appointed attorney, and I also worked full time at my job, as my family spent all extra hours organizing surgery for Israel, and hopefully for some ambulation for his right hip. The court-appointed attorney found no foul play in the attorneys' fees, but seemed surprised when I mentioned the three months spent in a nearby lodging that ate up nearly $60,000, excluding the cost of food. We went forward, leaving the conversation concerning the politics to less valuable time. We proceeded under the system that kept us from the necessary leisure time we needed to heal our grief and to seek further healing for our son. Israel went into surgery, under anesthesia for five hours, Feb. 28, 1996.

They scraped the heterotopic bone that wrapped itself like hardened seaweed around his right hip, that had a hairline fracture. They extended muscles in four places, inner thigh, under the knee, hamstrings in the right leg and the arch of the foot to flatten the effect of trophy, and the Achilles' heel. Some of my family came from Minnesota to support us, as I knew the dangers of putting a head injury patient under anesthesia; and my emotions reflexed back to his initial coma. But God was faithful and the next day we took him home. The pain was unbearable. Night and day he screamed as no medication for pain had any relief, and his agitation was violent and painful for us, like nothing you can run from. We prayed and massaged and talked to him day in and day out, all day, spoon-feeding him again due to the nauseous effect of the anesthesia. I returned to my nutritional regime with protein and acidophilus and healing herbs, while we comforted him with hot baths. We also slowly detoxed him off medications, building his own immune system. I took my mom back to the airport and the worst was over. Israel was alive and still recovering, all along realizing his losses, venting his anger and learning to heal by choice. God brought to my mind the social worker who had urged me to waive the conservatorship, and I was too busy and preoccupied to listen. I called him for a visit and urged my attorneys to prepare the paperwork.

It was June and the social worker's visit was supportive; he was the dragon slayer that we needed. There was no doubt in my mind that he was directed by angels. When the date for court arrived, our lawyer didn't have our paper work (the final documents prepared by this social worker) that ended the conservatorship. It was not necessary for his legal presence to be there. My husband nudged me as the attorneys stood dumbfounded and I handed them the copy I had received by mail. It was done! God was able and the attorneys were astounded that it was so easily passed. It would have been six more months to get a court date. Another miracle leading to freedom. We paid sixteen thousand dollars to local attorneys before the final separation from court attorneys for the family. God gave us the victory again, for Jesus said in the Scriptures, "I have overcome the world, and so shall ye! Greater is he that is you than he that is in the world."

8

Restoration

Margaret Ayer spent many hours on Israel on neurofeedback, taming the temper that was left from head injury for a small fee. A local alternative medicine M.D. used chelation therapy (or amino acid drip) to strengthen his nutrition and improve lean muscle. We did five treatments in the hyperbaric chamber for oxygen in Santa Monica, and continued to use supplements, including Piractecem from England, for brain stimulation for health. We took Israel to a Benny Hinn healing ministry and continued to attend church at Bethel Christian Center every Sunday.

Remarkable things happened at this small church. Our son began to find peace in Jesus Christ and a relationship that stabilized his life emotionally and spiritually. Michelle, our daughter, was on her third year at Westmont University and God was miraculously opening doors for her education and emotional health. George had managed to graduate from a local college as a medical assistant after attending one year, and Israel enrolled at Golden Grain Bible College. Israel spent hours on the phone and he went everywhere with a new enlightment of Jesus Christ. He shakes the marachas with his one hand to the music in the worship service in the church.

Israel has truly grown in his gift to love, and as his memory heals, he understands more and more the true freedom in life that begins in the spirit and flows out. He knows and understands that the name "Israel" has been a legend of blessing as stated in Genesis. He knows he has robbed death for life and hope to live. *Beyond Coma* is a book for people to touch the reality of a coma and a life that came beyond it, and a family that will run the race of life that is set before us.

As for our family, Israel's laughter heals the terror of silence that we knew so well, and the love of God was the power that took us through those caverns of despair. Today, we who have been witnesses to the miracle of Israel will have to face what we will do tomorrow with what we've learned from his miracle and his faith in Jesus Christ. Seasons have come and gone in this account of memory, and the song that I wrote, ("Send me red roses and I will wait till you do") lingers in my memory. Each time Mother's Day comes Israel asks me if I want roses, and I tell him, yes. I certainly do.

Afterword

It is now April of 1997, and at the completion of this book, Israel is walking on his feet with a four-prong cane. He walks up and down stairs and swims the full length of the pool with one arm. If you see him on the street, he'll speak to you as if you are an old friend. His values have changed since his commitment to Christ and he will tell you up-front that the Lord saved his life. His tenderness toward children and elderly people is the same as before and his flirting with ladies still continues.

His story is a miracle. He has no fungus, no pneumonia, no infections, and eats like a beast. His right hip continues to cause a limp, referring back to the Book of Genesis, when Jacob wrestled with the angel and his right hip was maimed for a testimony to the Lord. His social IQ keeps us like teenagers, and our hope is in the Lord. Nutritional and alternative medicine deserves much credit, for the many medical doctors and writers are changing the frontier in western medicine. I am grateful to them for helping in the restoration of my son.

I will continue to encourage others who have need of the knowledge that God has provided to help the body heal itself. God specializes in the entire human being, and Israel is only one life that is being restored in this story. God is restoring each life in this family, one day at a time. One of the most important ongoing miracles is the taming of the temper, in which God has been the guide and healer, because only He can change the heart.

The Life of Paul the Christian

I see Paul as a practical human being and he shows this through his testimony of how he was converted. People's spiritual sight is as blind as can be. Actually, people without the Lord's love are already dead. When the Lord wakes you up, you really can't believe that dealing with Him was so simple. So being a human being is actually a dysfunctional reality of life. But knowing the Lord brings peace and joy all around.

The Jews were against the Christians. The Holy Spirit would always be there. Sharing the good news with others is a major recovery. With the Holy Spirit's presence and power, we're able to deal with hard times and life itself.

Paul was born a Roman citizen who was down for the law. Paul depended on other folks for help and he traveled a lot. He was educated by Gameliel and is believed to have written many of the letters in the early church years. Paul went through three days of blindness, and his suffering made him find peace as the Lord was standing there watching his every move. His parents made sure that he grew up in the Jewish Church. The date of his conversion to Christianity was about 32 A.D.

Being forgiven for our sins will set us free from bondage from our past. It is simple. Paul chose on his own to look for his own beliefs. He checked out different religions and he traveled a lot. At his conversion, many Christians doubted his Christianity. Paul had the desire to keep the Gospel going forward. Paul, when compared to his teacher's personality, was the opposite. The testimony of Paul and the letters he wrote pushes us to move on. His letters make us want to keep on moving. Paul had a conscience and he had an idea that he wasn't going to be an ideal person. He describes the Lord as radiant light.

A lot of Christians were once prosecutors, but the Holy Spirit's presence made them wake up. Paul heard time and time again the Lord speak after being converted, and he had the desire for following other Christians. After seeing the light like Paul, anybody would go forward. The smooth thing is that Paul wasn't introduced to the Lord by any followers, but by the Lord, Himself. He went to many places and regions to tell many people about the love of Christ. His letters were full of the righteousness of Christ. His life was organized through the Lord and he was a servant of Christ, later becoming an Apostle. We all know he was zealous over the ways pertaining to Christ. He also joined Peter in Christianity.

Christians glorified God the Almighty for being the one and only to reach Paul's heart. He went to all the churches being established to enlighten them over and over again. There was rude opposition from the Jews, but he kept on spreading the Gospel to the Jews, even though the Jews had great opposition towards Christians. He felt that preaching to the Jews was a calling God placed on him.

It has been said that he thought carefully about his missionary work, and he really wanted to bring people into a relationship with Christ that would help them go forward. He appointed leaders in different churches as he travelled, and his belief in the meaning of the death of Jesus is the one thing that gets all Christians moving forward. Paul's belief in the power of the resurrection of Christ was powerful to the Christian church, then and now. By his letters, we understand that the return of Christ was to be of extreme hope. He suffered many beatings, imprisonments, and other hardships for Christ, and in the end, he was finally beheaded for the Lord. Paul was a smooth character.

Israel Echevarria